50

fantastic things to do with
a sand tray

KIRSTINE BEELEY & ALISTAIR BRYCE-CLEGG

Published 2012 by Featherstone Education
Bloomsbury Publishing plc
50 Bedford Square, London, WC1B 3DP
www.bloomsbury.com

ISBN 978-1-4081-5986-6

Text © Kirstine Beeley and Alistair Bryce-Clegg 2012
Design © Lynda Murray
Photographs © Shutterstock

Printed and bound in China by C&C Offset Printing Co Ltd, Shenzhen, Guangdong
10 9 8 7 6 5 4 3

This book is produced using paper that is made from wood grown in
managed, sustainable forests. It is natural, renewable and recyclable.
The logging and manufacturing processes conform to the environmental
regulations of the country of origin.

To see our full range of titles visit **www.bloomsbury.com**

Acknowledgements
We would like to thank the staff and children of the following settings for their time
and patience in helping to put this book together, including the use of a number of
photographs.

Acorn Childcare Ltd, Milton Keynes
Treehouse Preschool, Winslow, Bucks
Prestwood Infant School, Prestwood, Bucks
MKFocus Childcare Ltd, Milton Keynes
Penguin Preschool, Timperley, Cheshire
The Friars Primary School, Salford

Also special thanks to Fee Bryce-Clegg.

Contents

Introduction

Sand has long been established as a staple in early years provision. But just having a sand tray because 'we've always had it' is no longer sufficient when planning for individual children's learning and development. We need to embrace the wonderful array of experiences that sand can offer and recognise the many ways in which sand play can support learning and development across all areas of the EYFS framework.

Sand can broadly be viewed as having two main states - wet and dry. Each offers its own unique set of experiences and this book aims to look at how you can engage children in sand play to make the most of both of these superb learning opportunities. Dry sand offers pouring and tipping experiences on a variety of scales to build on children's physical and sensory development whilst wet sand offers a great way of exploring materials and how they change as children squish it, squeeze it or add other materials to it.

Sand provision should ideally be available daily in your setting and many of the ideas in this book offer solutions for smaller scale activities ideal when space is at a premium. You don't have to be using a full sized sand tray all of the time, it's more important to have some smaller sand provision than none at all!

Remember that sand play is not just for indoors and that outdoor play is of equal importance in early years provision. This book truly embraces the thinking that outdoor play should offer unique learning opportunities which are not necessarily possible or practical indoors. The outdoor activities here will help you to ensure that your outdoor sand play is truly 'outdoors' and NOT just your indoor sand play taken out through the door.

Always remember to follow good hygiene practices when adding food products or other materials to your sand and remember to sterilise your sand tray regularly to ensure no harmful germs get the opportunity to breed. With outdoor sand areas always make sure you can cover the area when not in use to prevent small animals using it as a litter tray and always check that the area is free from harmful objects before use.

We hope you will enjoy pouring, scooping, squishing and squeezing and most of all having fun learning!

Skin allergy alert

Some detergents and soaps can cause skin reactions.

Always be mindful of potential skin allergies when letting children mix anything with their hands and always provide lots of facilities to wash materials off after they have been in contact with the skin. Watch out for this symbol on the relevant pages!

Food allergy alert

When using food stuffs to enhance your sand play opportunities always be mindful of potential food allergies. We have used this symbol on the relevant pages.

Sand art plaques

What you need:

- A selection of shallow plastic plant pot saucers in a variety of shapes and sizes
- Some wet play sand
- A wide selection of interesting weather-proof objects including coloured glass beads, shells, stones, pebbles, wooden chips etc (don't use items such as conkers and acorns as these will rot and go mouldy over time)
- Plaster of Paris mix
- A container for mixing plaster which can be thrown away afterwards
- A stick for stirring plaster (Don't use your best mixing spoon!)
- A DIY paintbrush

What to do:

1. Select your plant pot saucer, fill the bottom of it with wet sand and press down to give a smooth surface.

2. Press objects into the wet sand to make your sand art patterns.

3. When you are happy with your sand art, (you can always take things out, smooth the sand and try again), mix up the Plaster of Paris according to the manufacturer's instructions. (This is an adult activity due to the heat generated during the mixing process).

4. Pour the plaster on to your sand art until the sand is completely covered.

5. Leave to harden.

6. When the plaster has cooled and hardened, tip out the plaster plaque and using a DIY paintbrush brush away the wet sand to reveal your sand art plaque.

Warning!

Never pour excess plaster of paris down the drain – it will block it!

Top tip ★

Mark the child's initials into the plaster as it starts to dry to help identify it later.

Taking it forward

- Make plaques on a big scale in seed trays or bin lids and fill with ready-mix cement to make sensory stepping stones for your outdoor area.

- Leave a selection of interesting objects out with some wet sand so children can explore making patterns and shapes by pressing them into the sand. (Glass beads are great for this but need adult supervision to avoid choking hazard).

What's in it for the children?

This activity offers the opportunity for the children to see first hand how some materials can change their appearance, texture and use when other materials are added to them.

Coloured rice

What you need:

- Some white rice
- Re-sealable plastic bags (one for each colour you make)
- A tablespoon
- White (clear) vinegar
- Some food colouring
- A mixing bowl (metal to avoid staining)
- Mixing spoons (metal to avoid staining)
- A baking tray lined with foil
- A measuring cup

What to do:

1. Measure your rice by the cup into a plastic bag. Put as little or as much as you want into the bag (make sure the bag is big enough to allow some shaking space).

2. Add one tablespoon of white vinegar to the bag for every cup of rice. (The vinegar helps the colour to bond to the rice. Without it you get 'patchy rice'.)

3. Add as much or as little food colouring as you need, depending on the depth of colour that you want. (You can always add more before you dry your rice.)

4. Shake the bag until all of the rice looks covered. If the colour isn't strong enough then add more food colouring and vinegar. The more you add, the easier it is to colour the rice but the longer it will take to dry.

5. Spread your rice onto a foil lined baking tray and leave to dry. In a warm spot it will usually dry in around three hours but to be sure, overnight is best.

Taking it forward

- There are many uses for coloured rice other than for texture play.

- Put several colours in the sand tray and let the children mix them up to make rainbow rice.

- Make pink 'fairy' rice and add sequins, glitter and flower petals for a sparkly small world experience.

- For an extra sensory element you can add flavouring essence to the rice in your tray.

What's in it for the children?

This activity offers the children an opportunity to experience different textures and also to experiment with how different materials behave in different ways depending on how they are made.

Popcorn factory

What you need:

- Popcorn kernels (uncooked)
- A variety of utensils such as scoops, pots, buckets and sieves
- Funnels and clear plastic tubes
- Popcorn maker or pan

What to do:

1. Initially use popcorn kernels uncooked in your sand tray.
2. Try different sized trays and containers to experience different depths of kernels.
3. Use funnels and tubes to move the kernels around the tray.
4. Cook the kernels in a popcorn maker or pan.
5. Allow the children to experiment with the new texture.
6. Provide a mixture of both cooked and uncooked popcorn.

Taking it forward

- Add other containers such as metal bowls and tins to create different sounds as the kernels move around.
- Can the children get the popcorn kernels into the popcorn machine using the funnels and tubes?
- Use lots of popped kernels on a large scale across the floor indoors or out.
- Hide objects at the bottom of the popcorn for the children to find.
- Provide darning needles (under adult supervision) and embroidery thread or wool so that the children can create long 'popcorn' strings.
- Add cardboard tubes and straws so that the children can experiment with using their breath to pick up or blow away the popped kernels.
- Provide egg boxes, fruit packing and small containers to encourage the children to sort.

What's in it for the children?

This activity offers the children an opportunity to experience different textures and also to experiment with how different materials behave in different ways. The 'popping' of the corn kernels shows children how heat can effect different materials and their properties.

Pine needles

What you need:

- Fresh pine needles
- Fir cones
- Bark
- Pestle and mortar

Alternative to pine needles

- Green rice (see page 7)
- Pine oil or fragrance

If you use rice this becomes more of a small world activity

What to do:

1. Give the children a mixture of pre-stripped pine needles and pine branches that will allow the children to pull the needles off.

2. Let the children crush the leaves between their fingers.

3. With supervision, they can crush the pine needles and bark using a pestle and mortar and release the amazing smell of pine.

Top tip ★

Use fresh pine as dead or dry needles can be sharp.

Taking it forward

- Even though this is primarily a sensory experience, you can link it to experiences children may be familiar with such as Christmas by adding enhancements like glitter pompoms, plastic baubles and Christmas themed small world resources.

- Create the illusion of snow (if it isn't snowing!) with powdered instant potato, fake snow or white rice.

- Provide the children with jars, bottles and water. Challenge them to make their own pine air freshener or aftershave/perfume.

What's in it for the children?

This activity offers the children an opportunity to experience a familiar object in a different way. The pine needles offer a different sensory experience depending on how they are handled.

Grow your own

What you need:

- Wet sand
- Beans and seeds
- A sunny, warm spot

Taking it forward

- Provide smaller trays and leave them for different lengths of time.

- Use a tray that is just dry sand. Do the seeds and beans change? (This doesn't work with compost unless the compost is completely dry.)

- Grow things that you can eat like mustard and cress to add another sensory dimension.

- Once your seeds have grown, provide small world resources to create habitats for imaginative play.

What's in it for the children?

Children have the opportunity to explore the differences between wet and dry sand. They can also see how the sand is able to remain wet and that moisture is essential for the seeds to grow. Lots of opportunities here for developing questioning language as well as knowledge of how seeds grow.

Top tip ⭐

This activity works really well with wet sand but if you fancy a change, fill your sand tray with compost before you start.

What to do:

1. Make sure that your sand is nice and wet.

2. Use a mixture of seeds and beans so that you can push some into the sand and scatter some on the top.

3. Choose some fast growers like mustard and cress and some slower ones like beans and grass.

4. Leave the tray in a sunny, warm spot.

5. Let the children predict what they think is going to happen. (DON'T TELL THEM THE ANSWER.)

6. If your sand is in a warm bright spot, you should get some growth within a couple of days.

7. Let the children dig and explore in the sand and find seeds and beans at different stages of development.

8. As well as being very tactile, this activity also has lots of opportunities for the children to experience smells!

Egg shells

What you need:

- **Egg shells** (as complete as possible)
- **An empty sand tray**
- **Kitchen utensils** to crush, mash and grind

What to do:

1. Wash your egg shells thoroughly before putting them in the tray.

2. Put the shells into your tray and let the children experiment with snapping and crushing them with the kitchen utensils.

3. Introduce different equipment that will encourage the children to break the shells down even further.

4. Keep all the bits of broken shell for the children to use in their next creative project.

Health & Safety
Make sure the children wash their hands thoroughly after this activity.

Taking it forward

- Add liquid to the crushed shells and observe any changes.

- Move the crushed shells to smaller containers and add drops of food colouring to provide coloured egg shells for your artwork.

- Put your crushed egg shells onto a mirror or light box to use for pattern making.

Big it up!

- Use a hair dryer (set to cool) for larger scale work.

- Blow up a balloon (hold it tightly) and use the expelling air to blow your paint.

What's in it for the children?

In this activity you are using a substance that most children will find really familiar and allowing them to explore it in a new and unique way. This activity provides lots of opportunities for language development too.

Top tip ⭐

To be extra safe you can bake your shells in a hot oven for 15 minutes to kill any germs.

FOOD allergy !

Flax seed

What you need:

- Flax seed
- Cups
- Bowls
- Funnels
- Tubing
- Small world resources

What to do:

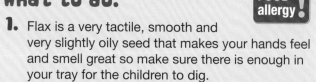

1. Flax is a very tactile, smooth and very slightly oily seed that makes your hands feel and smell great so make sure there is enough in your tray for the children to dig.

2. Flax seed is also very good for pouring and is often described as having the properties of 'dry water'. It's good for using with all of the resources that you would traditionally have in your water tray.

3. You could hide metal items in the bottom of your tray and give the children metal detectors or magnets to help them in their search.

4. Have access to small world resources available but let the children's interests and ideas lead which equipment you use.

Taking it forward

- Provide linking tubes, funnels and milk cartons with masking tape to create a pouring machine.

- Encourage the children to use descriptive language to tell you how the flax feels.

- You can also use other types of seeds in the same way. Large bags of mixed corn (for chickens) are easy to get hold of.

Top tip ⭐

If you add small amounts of warm water to the flax seed then eventually it will soften and take on a whole different texture.

What's in it for the children?

Flax seed has a very unusual and unique texture and is probably an unknown substance to most children. This activity provides great opportunities for language development particularly around questioning and description as well as a new sensory experience.

Coffee grounds

Top tip ⭐
Don't put coffee grounds down the sink or drain!

What you need:

- **Used coffee grounds** (from your coffee machine or cafetiere)
- **Sand tray**
- **Tubes**
- **Funnels**
- **Containers**
- **Small world characters**

FOOD allergy!

Taking it forward

- Add some whole coffee beans to the mix.

- Provide the children with a pestle and mortar and let them have a go at grinding a few beans of their own.

- Make glue trails on paper and then bury the paper in the coffee grounds. The grounds will stick to the glue to produce instant art!

- Use dry coffee grounds on a lightbox for interesting mark making.

- Coffee grinds are a great substitute for soil/mud when creating habitats for small world play.

What's in it for the children?

In this activity you are using a substance that most children will be aware of and allowing them to explore it in a new and unique way. This activity provides lots of opportunities for language development and experience of textures and smells.

What to do:

Dry coffee grounds

1. Dry out your coffee grounds by spreading them out on a baking tray and leaving to air-dry or put the tray into the oven at 120 degrees for 15 minutes.

2. Add the grounds to your sand tray while they are still warm and let the children dig their hands into them for both texture and smell.

3. When dry they are very good for pouring, sieving and funnelling.

Wet coffee grounds

1. Add small amounts of water to your coffee grounds and let the children mix (with their hands or utensils) and see what happens.

2. Damp grounds will work very much like wet sand so are really good for moulding, modelling and building.

3. Add lots of water to create a coffee/mud swamp that can be fished in or sieved to reveal hidden treasures.

4. Add corn flour to your swamp for a thick, grainy, gloop!

Coloured pasta

What you need:

- **Rubbing alcohol** (optional but it helps to increase the intensity of the colour and also speeds up the drying process)
- **Large sellable freezer bags**
- **Plain white pasta** (mixed shapes)
- **Food colouring**
- **Newspaper**

What to do:

1. Put a few drops of rubbing alcohol into your bag. (The amount depends on the size of the bag and the amount of paste you are going to use.)

2. Half fill your bags with pasta.

3. Add a few drops of food colouring (depending on the strength of colour you want).

4. Shake the bag well. If all of the pasta isn't coated add more colouring and rubbing alcohol.

5. Leave the pasta in the bag for a couple of hours giving it a good shake every time you walk past it.

6. Empty the contents of the bag onto thick newspaper and leave to dry.

7. Add the dry pasta to your sand tray and let the children experience the texture and sound as they move it around.

Taking it forward

- Add different lengths of ribbon and string to your tray so that the children can thread the pasta.

- Provide pots in the same colours as the pasta you have made so that the children can match and sort.

What's in it for the children?

This activity offers the children an opportunity to experience different textures and also to experiment with how different materials behave in different ways because of how they are made.

Top tip ★

The colouring process is just as exciting as the experience of playing with the end result, so do both with the children.

Quick sand

What you need:

- Sand container
- Sand
- Corn flour
- Water
- Food colouring (optional)

What to do:

1. Add one cup of sand to your sand container.

2. Add one cup of corn flour to the sand.

3. Add one cup of water to the mixture and stir.

4. Add food colouring to change the colour of your quicksand

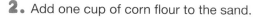

Taking it forward

- This activity is one that can be different every time you do it. The children will enjoy adding more dry ingredients and more water to get the consistency just right.

- You can add small world resources to turn this into a quicksand adventure.

- Encourage lots of pouring to see how the liquid changes.

- Try floating a variety of objects on the top of your quicksand and see which take longest to sink.

What's in it for the children?

Not only do the children have the opportunity to explore a variety of textures and smells but they also get to see first hand how mixing different substances together can change how they look and feel.

Metal detectors

What you need:

- A variety of metal objects
- Some scraps of fabric and paper
- A sand tray full of sand
- Hand held metal detectors
- A collecting bag or box
- Paper and pencils to record findings

What to do:

1. Bury a variety of metal objects in your sand tray.
2. Wrap some of the metal objects in fabric and paper to see if this makes a difference.
3. See how many objects the children can find.
4. Encourage the children to record what they have discovered (if appropriate).

Taking it forward

- Use wet and sand for a different digging experience.
- Wrap non-metallic items in tin foil and see if the children can explain why they have been able to find them.
- Take it outside on a larger scale and get the children to hide and discover 'buried treasure'

What's in it for the children?

There are lots of opportunities in this activity for children to explore some scientific concepts around metal and its properties. Also a good opportunity to develop questioning, predictive and descriptive language.

Making bricks

What you need:

- Sand
- Water
- PVA glue
- Yogurt pots, milk cartons, an ice cube tray

Taking it forward

- Use containers such as jelly moulds to make unusually shaped bricks.
- Add some powder paint to your mix before setting, for coloured bricks.
- Add compost/mud to the mixture and see what happens.
- Try using only compost/mud and no glue. Why does this work? How is it different?
- You can do this on a much larger scale in your outdoor sandpit – it will just take your bricks longer to dry.

What's in it for the children?

This is a great activity for letting children explore the (simplified) process of how a familiar object is made. They can also go on to use their bricks in their construction and small world play.

Top tip ⭐

Always do a 'test' brick that you can poke without ruining anyone's hard work!

What to do:

1. If you are starting with dry sand, add water a little at a time and stir until the sand is damp but not soaked.

2. Stir in a good squirt of PVA glue. (This doesn't have to be exact and depends on how much sand you have. It's always better to have more than less!)

3. If your mixture is getting too sloppy add more dry sand. It should have the same texture as wet sand.

4. You can also add chopped up straw or dried grass into the mixture at this stage to help to hold your bricks together.

5. Pack the mixture into whatever containers you have chosen.

6. Leave to dry. Remember the deeper/bigger your container, the longer it will take to dry. An ice cube tray of mini-bricks should dry overnight. A yogurt pot might take 3 or 4 days.

Sand tray mystery

What you need:

- **A large piece of cardboard** (big enough to fit across the top of your sand tray)
- **Sand tray**
- **Different sized shapes to draw around**
- **Craft knife or scissors**

Taking it forward

- For more permanent use, use wood instead of cardboard.

- For individual children or smaller groups try this with a washing up bowl or smaller tray.

- Use the activity for language development, not only of children's descriptive language but also naming and labelling.

What's in it for the children?

This is like a 'blind' challenge for the children that requires them to rely on their sense of touch and their knowledge of texture to try and work out what they're feeling in the tray. As they cannot show you what it is, it's a great opportunity to develop their descriptive language.

Top tip ⭐

The idea is that the children cannot see what is in the sand tray but will put their hands through the holes and see what they find!

What to do:

1. Make sure your card is big enough to cover the top of your tray.

2. Cut a variety of different size and shaped holes in the card.

3. Make the holes big enough for the children to get their hands through but not so big that they can see into the tray.

4. Put some holes close together so that they can use two hands at once.

5. Fill the tray with interesting textures and/or buried objects.

6. Get the children to put their hands through the holes and talk about what they think they have found.

7. Either get the children to pull out the object they find to see if they were right or leave it in to maintain the mystery for other children!

Chalk and sandpaper

What you need:

- Dry sand
- Chalk in a variety of colours and sizes
- Sandpaper in a variety of thicknesses
- Water
- Eye droppers or turkey basters

What to do:

1. Start with dry sand.
2. Rub the chalk against the sandpaper to create coloured dust.
3. Create piles of chalk dust.
4. Add drops of water to some of the piles and see how they change.
5. Mix some of the dust into the sand.
6. Add drops of water to the dust and sand mixture so see the colour change.

Taking it forward

- Try dampening the sandpaper with a wet paintbrush and see the effect it has on the chalk when you rub it.
- Soak some of the chalk in water before you use it and talk about the differences.
- Try with lots of different gradients of sand paper. Does it make a difference?

What's in it for the children?

This activity offers a different textural experience to sand. It also shows the children some of the different properties of chalk. If you use a number of colours then there will be lots of opportunities to discuss colour mixing too.

Sand putty

What you need:

- Corn flour
- PVA Glue
- Sand
- Water
- Mixing bowl
- Sand tray
- Food colouring

What to do:

1. Mix 1 cup of corn flour and half a cup of PVA glue together.
2. Add the corn flour mix to 2 cups of sand.
3. Stir or mix with hands.
4. If it's too sticky add more sand and if it is too dry add more water.
5. Add food colouring if required.
6. Leave overnight.

Taking it forward

- Rather than mixing this in a bowl, have a go at mixing it in the tray with the children so that they can see all of the changes that take place.

- You can add other items to your putty such as colours, flavours and textures.

- This putty is really good for developing children's fine motor dexterity.

What's in it for the children?

This activity allows children to combine substances together to see how they change to create a new substance. They can experiment with how adding more or less of one substance can change the constancy and texture of the mixture.

Top tip ★

The starch in the corn four removes the moisture from the glue leaving it more like a putty than a dough.

Sandscape

What you need:

- Damp sand
- A sand tray
- A variety of tubes of different widths and lengths
- A variety of containers
- A selection of small balls (ping-pong balls are ideal)
- Drinking straws

What to do:

1. Using damp sand allows the children to build and mould a variety of 'hills' and 'valleys' into the sand tray.

2. Build some of the 'hills' around containers to create caves.

3. Make some of the 'hills' over tubes to create tunnels.

4. Once the landscape is complete, challenge the children to move a ping-pong ball from one side of the tray to the other visiting as many caves and tunnels along the way as they can.

5. Use the drinking straw to suck and blow their ball (not the sand!)

Taking it forward

- You could add numbers to the holes and caves to create a version of crazy golf.
- Take it outside in your sand or digging pit and use drainpipes, carpet inner tubes and larger balls.

What's in it for the children?

While moulding the sand to house their tubes or creating 'sand caves' the children are developing their gross and fine motor skills as well as their hand eye coordination and thinking skills.

Top tip ⭐

Show the children how to stick their ball to the end of the straw by sucking. This will help them to move the ball when it gets stuck.

Spray paint sand

What you need:

- Dry sand
- Food colouring
- Water
- Hand-held water spray/ mister (or water guns for extra fun)
- Sand

Taking it forward

- Change the setting on the nozzle of your spray for different effects.
- Add a solution of paint and water to the spray instead of food colouring.
- Take it outside into your sand pit for some large-scale art.
- Use old washing up liquid bottles instead of spray bottles to create stronger lines.

What's in it for the children?

This activity shows how water changes the consistency and texture of sand. The addition of colour adds an extra dimension related to colour recognition and mixing. The use of a spray or mister helps children to develop their fine motor skills as well as their hand/ eye coordination through their aim.

Top tip ★

This activity works on both wet and dry sand but the colours are brighter if the sand is wet.

What to do:

1. Half fill the spray with water.
2. Add drops of food colouring until you achieve the right strength of colour.
3. If the colour is too weak add more food colouring, if it is too strong add more water.
4. Spray the coloured water onto the sand to create patterns and change the texture.
5. When the upper layer of sand is damp, rake it over and start again.

Match it

What you need:

- **Sand** (wet or dry)
- **Construction kit** (like Duplo)
- **Example cards**
- **Sand timer**

What to do:

1. Create simple models using a construction kit.
2. Photograph your model and laminate it to make an example card.
3. Bury a variety of your chosen construction kit in the sand.
4. The children choose an example card and then dig in the sand to find all of the pieces they need to build what they see.

Taking it forward

- You can increase the difficulty of the activity by:
  - making a more complex example
  - hiding more construction pieces
  - doing the activity against the clock by using a sand timer
  - taking this idea outside but using large scale construction pieces rather than small

What's in it for the children?

This activity is a test of memory, matching and dexterity. The children will be developing all of these skills at the same time as they find the blocks, match them to the original model and then create a version of their own.

Peas, rice and beans

What you need:

- Dry sand
- A sand tray
- Dried peas
- Uncooked rice
- A variety of dried pulses like lentils and beans
- A variety of sieves and colanders of different sizes
- Spoons, ladles and containers

What to do:

1. You can add all of the peas, beans and rice at once or add them one at a time.

2. Ask the children to use the sieves and colanders to see if they can separate different combinations of peas, beans and rice.

3. Can they find the sieve that will just give them beans?

4. Can they find the colander that will give them peas and beans?

Taking it forward

- For a different texture experience, add the peas, beans and rice first to the sand tray and let the children experience them before adding the sand.

- Use the containers to collect and sort the pulses.

- Can the children make/find other ways of sorting peas, rice and beans?

What's in it for the children?

Alongside the different textures of the different pulses, this activity allows children to experiment with shape, size and capacity as they try and sort the mixed ingredients in the tray by size and shape.

Top tip ★

Make sure your sand is 'bone' dry or the dried peas and beans will begin to germinate and smell!

Sand creatures

What you need:

- Damp sand
- Sand tray
- Dry paint brushes (various sizes)
- Sand trowels
- Plastic knives and spoons
- Variety of collage materials

What to do:

1. Encourage the children to shape the sand with their hands to create mounds and shapes.

2. Use the brushes and modelling tools to experiment with sculpting and shaping their mounds.

3. Add collage material to create hair, eyes, scales, claws, whatever they would like their creature to have.

Taking it forward

- Depending on the children's stage of development, you can introduce them to different ways of using the tools to create patterns and shapes.

- Start by creating a sand creature that looks like it is lying down. Then try one standing up.

- Take it outside and re-create on a large scale using natural materials to add to your sand sculpture.

What's in it for the children?

This activity encourages children to use their creativity and imagination to create a sand creature. It also provides opportunities to use familiar objects from other areas of the setting (indoors and out) to enhance their creation.

Sand trails

What you need:

- **Containers** (such as milk cartons, washing up liquid bottles)
- **Plastic freezer bags**
- **Sand**
- **Pegs**
- **Plain or coloured sand**

What to do:

1. With the children, make different sized holes into the bottom of a variety of containers.

2. Take your plastic bags and cut off one of the bottom corners. Cut a small amount off in some and a larger amount in others. The bigger the hole, the more sand will come out.

3. Fill the containers and the bags with sand.

4. Use a peg to close the holes in the bag until the children are ready to go.

5. Get the children to move around in the outside area whilst the sand pours out of their bag or container to create a trail.

6. Try different movements like hopping, running or turning in a circle.

Taking it forward

- Attach the container to the back of a wheeled toy and make a trail by riding.
- This can be done on a much smaller scale with a small container/bag and a builder's tray.
- Try replacing the sand with other textures like rice, sawdust or porridge.
- Create trails for children to follow and then ask them to do the same for you.

What's in it for the children?

This is a great opportunity for the children to develop balance and coordination. During this activity you could also concentrate on children's knowledge of pattern and positional language.

Baked cotton wool balls

What you need:

- Flour
- Water
- Food colouring
- Cotton wool balls
- Greaseproof paper
- Baking tray
- Oven
- Sand tray

Taking it forward

- Experiment with different sized balls of cotton wool.

- Wrap the cotton wool around a small object before you dip it, then when the children break it open they will find something inside.

- Hide a secret message inside the cotton wool before you dip it and bake for the children to discover.

What's in it for the children?

This shows the children an example of how combining different substances together can change them and how applying heat to that substance can change it from a liquid into a solid. There is also lots of opportunity to explore texture, sound and problem solving e.g. How are they going to find out what's inside?

What to do:

1. Mix the flour and water together until you get a paste that is the thickness of double cream (don't worry about the lumps!).

2. Add food colouring until you get the colour of your choice. If you want several colours then split your paste into separate containers and add a different colour to each.

3. Dip the cotton wool balls into the coloured paste (knock off any excess).

4. Place the covered cotton wool balls onto a baking tray lined with greaseproof paper.

5. Bake in the oven at 200 degrees for 45 minutes.

6. Take out and leave to cool.

7. Once cooled put into the sand tray and let the children break open the hard shells to reveal the soft fluffy insides.

Top tip ★

The cotton wool balls will be hard when they are baked. The children will need to try various utensils to help them to break them.

Sand city

What you need:

- Large outdoor sand space
- Buckets and spades
- Brushes
- Modelling tools
- Small world play

What to do:

1. Encourage the children to use the tools to mould the sand to create houses, shops, roads, hills and other natural and man-made features of the environment.

2. The children can enhance their small-scale model with flowers, twigs, grass and other natural products.

3. Introduce different elements of small world play into the environments that the children have created.

Taking it forward

- You could keep this as a longer-term project and expand the city into a farm, a harbour or a rescue centre.

- Encourage the children to use other areas of the environment to find and create their own small world props.

- Introduce the children to the use of a simple video camera and let them make their own 'Sand City' movies.

What's in it for the children?

There are lots of opportunities for large-scale movement. As the children dig in the sand they will be helping to develop their upper body strength and balance. This activity is perfect for small world play that will develop the children's imagination and language.

Sand kitchen

What you need:

- Large outdoor sand space
- Sand (wet and dry)
- Boxes
- Crates
- Pans
- Kitchen utensils
- Bowls, cups and plates

What to do:

1. Set up a kitchen role-play in or around part of your outdoor sand area.

2. Encourage the children to pour, stir, cook and bake using both wet and dry sand.

3. Let the children enhance their kitchen role-play with other natural objects that they can find in the outdoor space such as flowers, twigs and stones.

Taking it forward

- Make a sand kitchen a permanent feature of your outdoor space that allows children to experience the use of large-scale sand through a familiar role-play scenario.

- Add water to the sand and introduce a wide range of resources in various sizes to maintain interest and challenge.

What's in it for the children?

With a sand kitchen you are using a very familiar role-play setting to encourage children to explore all of the properties of wet and dry sand through mixing and pouring.

Bark, twigs and sticks

What you need:

- Play bark
- Empty sand tray
- Tree bark
- Small twigs
- Large sticks
- Straw/grass

What to do:

1. Fill your tray with play bark.
2. Add various lengths and thicknesses of twigs and sticks.
3. Add other pieces of tree bark for texture.
4. Add some lengths of straw and/or long grass for both texture and binding.
5. Encourage the children to experience the texture of the bark chips by using their hands to dig and pile.
6. The children can use the sticks to create shapes, patterns and sculptures.

Health & Safety

Consideration should be given to the possible risk of splinters and use of sharp objects.

Taking it forward

- Try this on a larger scale in your outdoor area by choosing larger sticks and grasses.
- You could link this activity to both indoor and outdoor small world habitat play.
- Use this activity to reflect children's interests and observations of the world around them such as bird's nests.

What's in it for the children?

Use this activity to reflect children's interests and observations of the world around them such as bird's nests. It also allows them to investigate familiar objects in a way they might not have done before.

Baking bonanza

What you need:

- Tray of play sand
- Warm water
- **Selection of baking equipment** - include silicon cake cases, muffin trays, spoons, spatulas, whisks, piping bags, mixing bowls, jugs, jelly moulds etc.
- **Selection of cake toppings** - include things like hundreds and thousands, silver cake baubles, etc
- Cake cases
- **Chef's aprons and hats for added play effect!**

What to do:

1. Add water to the sand to make a wet but moldable mix.
2. Encourage children to mix and make using the baking equipment.
3. Enjoy making and mixing and using the moulds and cake cases.
4. More water can be added to make a sloppy sand mixture, which can be piped through piping bags. Why not try the mixture for sand mousse on page 62?
5. Use sprinkles to give your creations added cupcake appeal!

Taking it forward

- Make up coloured icing using corn flour, water and food colouring and use to 'ice' your sand creations.
- Try colouring some sand beforehand and baking mulit-coloured 'cakes'.
- Use bread baking tins and large cake cases to try outside on a much bigger scale, add extra long wooden spoons (you can get them up to 1 metre long!) for extra mixing fun.

What's in it for the children?

This is a great way of embracing the interests of children who may otherwise shy away from messy play. As well as lots of hands-on sensory experience of the sand mixture, the baking moulds lead to using mathematical language.

Beach in a barrel

What you need:

- **A half oak barrel** (available online or from garden centres)
- **Dry sand**
- **Shells**
- **Pebbles**
- **Seaweed** (pond weed can be used if you can't get seaweed)

Taking it forward

- Add water and seaweed to the barrel, how does that feel on their feet now?

- Build a big beach in your outdoor sand area complete with beach towels, parasols, buckets, spades and beach balls.

What's in it for the children?

As well as experiencing the feel of the sand between their toes, this activity is great for encouraging talking and listening in small groups due to the way children sit in the barrel. It can be used as a permanent addition to your outdoor setting (great for those settings with limited space).

Top tip ★

To stop your beach barrel being used as a litter tray for local cats and wildlife, make sure you cover it overnight. The sand can be recycled afterwards as a garden planter for vegetables or herbs.

What to do:

1. Put about 15cm of sand in the bottom of the barrel. Add in shells and pebbles.

2. Encourage two or three children to take off their shoes, sit on the edge of the barrel with their feet in the sand.

3. Ask them to explore the sand with their toes and feet, what does it feel like, do they like it? What can they find in their 'beach in a barrel'?

As only two or three children can use this activity at a time (dependent on the size of the barrel) it is great for encouraging sharing and co-operative play. Make sure that children understand the rules of use and it doesn't revert to another sand tray just for digging in.

Digging for dinosaurs

What you need:

- A tray of dry sand
- A selection of different sized bone-shaped dog biscuits
- A selection of small spades
- Small brushes - paint brushes, DIY paint brushes and toothbrushes
- Magnifying glasses
- Dinosaur related books

What to do:

1. Bury the bone biscuits in the sand prior to the activity.

2. Talk to the children about dinosaurs and discuss how we know that they existed (because people called paleontologists dig up fossils and fossilized bones).

3. Explain that they are going to dig for dinosaur bones in the sand tray and that they have to be really careful not to break any of the bones so they will need to brush away the sand and dig really carefully.

4. Encourage children to look carefully using the magnifying glasses and then dig for the buried bones using the brushes and small spades.

5. When they find a bone, ask them to talk about what kind of dinosaur they think it has come from, use books to look at dinosaurs and discuss their size, habits etc.

Taking it forward

- You could make this activity even more exciting by burying a small animal skull which has been prepared properly (available from specialists).

- Bury a selection of bones outdoors in your digging area and have a large-scale outdoor dinosaur dig.

- Bury other objects like bottles and bits of pot etc. so that the children can have an archaeological dig.

- Add fossils to your sand tray for added discovery and discussion.

What's in it for the children?

The unique child is a cornerstone of EYFS delivery and this activity is a great way of combining young children's fascination with dinosaurs with the experience of digging, finding and moving objects within the sand tray. Imaginative play which embraces children 's interests will lead to loads more speaking and listening and will see children so much more engaged in their learning.

Top tip ⭐

Don't put bone biscuits into wet sand or they will go soggy!

Build it up

What you need:

- **Large outdoor sand area**
- **Water**
- **Bricks** (real or play)
- **Corn flour**
- **Selection of construction site role-play equipment** (high visibility jackets, hard hats, cones, signs etc.)
- **Trowels and spades** (preferably real full sized - not plastic play ones)
- **Plastic garden trugs and buckets for mixing cement**
- **Builder's tray**

Taking it forward

- Add some straw, sticks and pig masks to your construction area and see if you can rebuild the three pig's houses. Adding sticks and straw to your cement mix allows lots of texture and materials exploration as well as sensory stimulation.

- Try making your own bricks with mud and sand (see page 18).

What's in it for the children?

Playing with sand outdoors offers lots of unique opportunities to work on a much bigger scale and to use physical skills such as digging and moving that just cannot be accessed indoors on a smaller scale. As with all role-play opportunities outside, you should be looking to provide experiences that embrace the uniqueness of the outdoor environment.

What to do:

1. Mix up some cement (corn flour, water and sand) to whatever consistency you require (a runnier mixture is great for using with bricks to build walls, a drier mixture can be molded). You can mix you cement in garden trugs with sticks or on a builder's tray with big spades (as real builders do!).

2. Explore mixing, moving and building with your sand-cement mixture whilst encouraging lots of imaginative play and discussion around the building site.

Health & Safety
Always take the opportunity to point out good safe practice around building sites.

Top tip ★
Having water available in a plastic camping water container with a tap makes water instantly accessible for children to use with their mixtures without having to go back and forth to a tap.

Buckets and spades

What you need:

- **Tray of wet** (but not soggy) **sand**
- **Selection of coloured ice cream spoons** (available cheaply online)
- **Selection of plastic bottle tops and lids** (include milk bottle tops, fabric softener lids etc.)
- **Wooden cocktail sticks** (with the points cut off)
- **Sticky labels**

What to do:

1. Work with the children to show them how they can use the small spades (ice cream spoons) and buckets (bottle tops) to make miniature sandcastles.

2. Use the cocktail sticks and sticky labels to make flags for your sand castles.

3. Can the children make a sandcastle tower with the biggest at the bottom?

Taking it forward

- Encourage children to make different sized sandcastles, talk about big, bigger, biggest and see if they can make a row of sandcastles from large to small. Can they make sand castle patterns (e.g. big, small, big, small etc.)?

- Use coloured flags to make patterns (e.g. red, blue, red, blue). Can the children carry on the pattern?

- Use flags with numbers on. Can the children make the right number of sandcastles to go with the flag? Can they make a row of sandcastles and put the numbers in order?

- Use flags with letters on. Can the children tell you what sound the letter makes? Can they put flags together to make their name or very simple words? Bury objects in the sand. Can children dig up objects to go with the lettered flags?

What's in it for the children?

It's important that children are able to explore familiar situations with a slightly unfamiliar twist. This activity is great for really getting the concept of size across as children play with the extra small tools, as well as being a lovely way of building on hand-eye coordination and concentration skills.

Dinosaur swamp

What you need:

- A tray of dry sand
- A bottle of washing up liquid (hypoallergenic is best)
- Warm water
- Green food colouring
- A collection of leaves, twigs, moss, rocks, pebbles and other swamp like bits
- A selection of toy dinosaurs

What to do:

1. Add a large amount of the washing up liquid to the sand (at least half a bottle).
2. Mix in water a little at a time and stir well until you get a swampy frothy mix.
3. Add green food colouring to make your sand swampy.
4. Include rocks, leaves, twigs trees and moss to create your swamp.
5. Add dinosaurs and enjoy stomping them through the slimy swamp.

Taking it forward

- Try making up a swampy mix in a shallow tray (unused cat litter tray is ideal) and just allow the children to explore with their feet (without shoes and socks of course!) stomping through their own swamp.

- Make the same mix but different colours ...blue would make a great enhancement for an underwater small world play session or red for an alien planet experience.

What's in it for the children?

This is a great sensory experience which needs to be visited and revisited for children to build on their existing knowledge of how materials look, feel and behave. Putting this within the context of dinosaurs gives it a familiarity which will hopefully engage children more readily as they build lots of new brain connections.

DIY sand drawing boxes

What you need:

- A selection of shallow trays (tea trays are ideal)
- Coloured and shiny papers
- Scissors
- **Extra fine coloured sand** (available from educational suppliers). **Alternatively colour some fine play sand with food colouring and allow to dry.**
- **A selection of soft brushes and tools** (include cotton buds, pant brushes, paint sponges etc)

What to do:

1. Place the tray onto one of your selected papers and draw around the base.
2. Cut around the shape so that you have a cut out which fits exactly into the base of the tray - stick it down with tape or tack if needed.
3. Pour some coloured fine sand on top of the paper so there is a fine covering.
4. Enjoy using the tools and brushes to move the sand around in patterns to reveal the coloured paper underneath.

Taking it forward

- Try replacing your coloured paper with tin foil or a Perspex mirror to get a reflective pattern in your sand.
- Add coloured glass beads to your sand patterns for added creativity.
- Try hiding a picture under the sand and ask children to try guessing what it is as they move the sand with their tools.
- Line your tray with a sheet showing lots of pictures of objects beginning with a certain sound, can the children identify the pictures as they uncover them?
- Try on a much bigger scale but covering the bottom of a builders tray with nice coloured wrapping paper and adding fine sand and big DIY brushes.

Top tip ★

Avoid using coloured play sand on light boxes as it will scratch the surface.

What's in it for the children?

The sensory appeal of dry sand, especially fine dry sand is timeless. This activity gives children the chance to build on sensory experiences at the same time as providing opportunities to be creative as they explore mark making and letter/number formation.

Fairy rice

What you need:

- **Pink coloured rice** (see Coloured rice page 7)
- **A sand tray**
- **Craft flower petals** (or real if available)
- **Glitter and sequins**
- **Fairy figures**
- **Scoops, spoons and bowls**
- **Miniature tea set**

What to do:

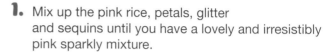

1. Mix up the pink rice, petals, glitter and sequins until you have a lovely and irresistibly pink sparkly mixture.

2. Add fairy figures and spoons, scoops etc for lots of pouring and sorting fairy play.

3. Add a miniature tea set for added fairy play excitement.

Taking it forward

- Make tiny fairy letters and leave for the children to read, provide lots of small pieces of paper and pens so they can reply!
- Add paper sweet bags for scooping and transporting your fairy mix.
- Use sieves and tea strainers to see if you can separate the 'fairy dust' from the pink rice.
- At Christmas why not try green rice, baubles, glitter stars and pompoms for a festive sand tray activity?

What's in it for the children?

This is definitely an activity for your lovers of all things pink and sparkly! As an alternative to dry sand activities it offers lots of pouring, sieving and filling whilst drawing on an imagination-filled fairy world full of talk and storytelling. Using small pots and bags encourages lots of mathematical talk about filling, empty, big, small etc.

Frozen sandcastles

What you need:

- Sand
- Water
- A selection of buckets, cups and pots
- A tray of sand
- Access to a freezer

What to do:

1. Mix up the sand with water until you have the right consistency to make sandcastles (make the mixture wetter rather than drier).

2. Fill a number of different shaped play buckets, pots, cups and jelly moulds with the wet sand mix.

3. Place in the freezer over night (during really cold weather the containers can be left outside over night to freeze).

4. When frozen, remove from the buckets and moulds and let the children explore the frozen sandcastles: How do they feel? Look?

5. What happens as the water in the sandcastles begins to melt?

Taking it forward

- Try using coloured water before you freeze your sandcastles.

- Place your frozen sandcastles in your outdoor sand area in both cold winter conditions and hot summer sun.

- Try making big frozen sandcastles in outdoor areas in winter.

What's in it for the children?

In order for learning to continue and move forwards, practitioners need to offer opportunities to challenge children's established thoughts and ideas. This activity allows them to revisit a familiar material (sand) in an unfamiliar state (frozen) and makes an exciting starting point for lots of early scientific observations and discussion (especially when the water which is frozen in between the sand particle starts to melt).

In the bag

What you need:

- A tray of dry sand
- A selection of different sized and coloured paper bags including lunch bags and sweet bags (these can be purchased really cheaply from online auction sites)
- A selection of spoons, scoops and cups
- A set of balance scales

What to do:

1. Explore filling the different sized bags with sand using all the scoops and spoons.

2. Explore their weight using the balance scales. Which is heaviest? Which is lightest? Is the bag full or empty? What happens if you add another bag or use a smaller or bigger bag?

3. Try revisiting using wet rather than dry sand - what happens to the bags when they get wet?

Taking it forward

- Try lots of different sorts of scales and balances.

- Use rice or lentils instead of sand to fill the bags.

- Experiment with boxes of different shapes and sizes instead of the bags.

- Try to use big present bags in your outdoor sand digging area for a bigger scale filling and weighing activity.

Remember to try and compost your bags after use or dry and put in your paper recycling bin.

What's in it for the children?

As well as being lots of fun, this activity has a strong mathematical slant with its exploration of concepts such as weight (heavy, heavier, light, lighter etc.) and capacity (full, fuller, empty). It also offers a great opportunity to introduce the correct use of scales and balances within the context of a fun and unusual exploration.

Lunar sand

What you need:

- A tray or bowl
- 6 cups of play sand
- 3 cups of corn flour
- 1 ½ cups warm water
- Food colouring

For larger quantities just adjust the amounts accordingly.

What to do:

1. Add the sand to a tray or bowl.
2. Fold in the corn flour with your hands.
3. Add water a little at a time until you get the desired texture (dry but clumps together when you squeeze it).
4. Mix in a small amount of food colouring for added effect.
5. Allow children to explore with their fingers and a selection of spades, spoons and other sand tools.

Taking it forward

- Make up lunar sand in lots of different colours and use as a base for small world imaginative play in a shallow tray on the floor or outdoors (green or red for a space planet exploration, blue for sea creatures and black for witches brew of plastic spiders and bugs).
- Add scents such as orange, lemon or peppermint food essence for a multi-sensory exploration.
- Add some sequins or glitter to the mix for added sparkly appeal.

What's in it for the children?

This mixture is a great alternative to the traditional play dough for building up muscles in hands and wrists (vital for early mark making and pencil control). The unusual stickiness of the mixture will challenge children's perceptions of sand and build vital brain connections as it stimulates those all important senses.

46

Magical mixtures

What you need:

- White vinegar/ lemon juice
- Food colouring
- Water
- Clear plastic bottles
- Sand
- Corn flour
- Bicarbonate of soda
- Glitter and sequins
- A selection of scoops, spoons and sticks for stirring
- Cups, jugs and bowls for mixing (ideally a plastic cauldron - available at Halloween from supermarkets)
- Droppers, pipettes and plastic water play syringes (not mentioned)
- Small bowls
- Selection of witch/wizard dressing up clothes

What to do:

1. Mix up some solutions of vinegar and/or lemon juice and water with various different food colourings and pour into the clear plastic bottles (available cheaply from pound shops and supermarkets).

2. Place the sand, corn flour, bicarbonate of soda, glitter and sequins into various small bowls.

3. Encourage children to mix up their own sand mixtures in the cauldron or a mixing bowl as part of role-playing wizards and witches potion making. Encourage lots of talk about what happens and what they see, smell, touch etc.

Taking it forward

- Link mixture making to stories such as 'What's in the Witches' Kitchen?' by Nick Sharratt or 'Memory Bottles' by Beth Shoshan for added mixing excitement.

- Create a mixture-making area outside where children can freely mix sand, water, mud etc - include camping kettles and saucepans as well as lots of sticks for stirring.

What's in it for the children?

Sand is great because it offers lots of ways to scoop, dig and mix. When added to other ingredients the way that these processes can be carried out changes along with the texture and properties of the sand. This activity allows children to explore these ever-changing properties by mixing up their own sand mixtures within the context of some fun and exciting magical role-play.

Minature magic

What you need:

- A tray of dry play sand
- A selection of small scale containers and scooping equipment - include tiny shampoo bottles (the sort you get in hotels or travel sets)
- Small spoons and tiny scoops (the smaller the better - plastic ice cream spoons are great and can be bought really cheaply on online)
- Tiny brushes
- Tea strainers and other small scale sieving equipment
- A selection of small containers (lids from bottles are great especially ones from milk and fabric conditioner bottles as they are brightly coloured too)

What to do:

1. Offer children a selection of small-scale sand equipment as an alternative to the usual buckets, spades and scoops.

2. Explore the wonders of dry sand play using tiny equipment.

Taking it forward

- Use extra fine sand (available from educational suppliers in a wide range of colours) for added pouring/sieving fun. Try pouring the sand onto a light box or mirrored surface for extra sensory enjoyment.

- Place some sand and small equipment in a gravel tray on the floor and allow children to sit around it (or even in it) as they explore the small scale equipment.

- Try tiny equipment with wet sand and make lots of miniature sandcastles.

- Why not go to the opposite extreme and have REALLY big equipment in your outdoor sand digging area - use full sized DIY buckets and spades, plastic garden trugs and big garden soil sieves.

What's in it for the children?

Using small scale tools and implements gives children a chance to revisit and build on their existing understanding of the properties of sand as well as giving loads of opportunity to develop and build on their finer motor skills and hand eye co-ordination as they try to fill with tiny spoons and scoops. Familiar activities in a tiny (or giant) scale can inject some added excitement and interest to your continuous provision.

Salt not sand

What you need:

- A couple of big bags of table salt
- A sand tray
- Scoops, spoons, sieves and sand wheels
- Food colouring

Taking it forward

- Make up coloured salt, put into bottles and pour over a layer of white salt to make patterns.

- Add sequins and sparkles to the salt and see if the children can get them out using sieves and tea strainers.

- Add some water to the salt - does it behave differently to sand?

What's in it for the children?

The opportunities that sand offers to pour, dig, scoop etc can also be offered by a wide selection of other materials - salt is only one, the fine granules of salt give it a unique pouring quality and an unusual texture on the hands.

Top tip

If you've got space in your freezer why not freeze a big tub of real snow for use later in the year!

What to do:

1. Add the bags of salt to the sand tray and allow children to explore in the same ways they would with sand. Encourage pouring, digging, scooping and sieving.

2. Although children find using, pouring and digging with white materials fascinating to vary the activity salt can be coloured by adding food colouring and then leaving to dry out again.

Health & Safety

Always ensure that salt is not eaten and that children's hands are free from scratches before playing in salt.

Putting a sock in it!

What you need:

- Sand in a tray
- Water
- A selection of socks in different sizes, colours and shapes - include adult, child and baby socks
- A selection of tights and pop socks
- Scoops and spoons
- Washing line and pegs

What to do:

Part 1: Dry sand

1. Encourage the children to fill the socks and tights with sand. Which can they fill the most? Which is biggest? Which is smallest? Which one is heaviest etc?

2. Include a few socks with holes in to add to the excitement.

Part 2: Wet sand

1. Now repeat the exploration using wet sand. Is it easier/harder to fill the socks with wet sand? The wet sand inside the socks and tights feels very different to the dry sand as it can be moulded and squashed much more easily.

2. Can they peg the socks full of sand to a washing line in order of size?

Taking it forward

- Try taking this activity outside on a really big scale and using large Christmas stockings, spades and buckets and a washing line with pegs.

- Try filling the socks with other materials that can be poured such as rice or salt.

- Outside (and under close adult supervision) can you swing the sand filled tights around? If you let go what will happen? Whose sand sock will go the furthest?

What's in it for the children?

This is a lovely activity for offering early science and maths exploration within the context of something fun and unusal. Children will be able to explore mathematical language surrounding weight, length and size as well as being able to squeeze, squash and squeeze as they discover more about the differing properties of wet and dry sand.

Pirate treasure hunt

What you need:

For map making

- Teabags
- Water
- A4 white paper

For treasure hunting

- A selection of costume jewellery bracelets, necklaces etc (available cheaply from charity shops or a plea to parents) **include some plastic coins**
- Spades and scoops
- Pirate hats/costumes

What to do:

1. Create your treasure map.

2. Place a teabag (or two) into a bowl and add warm water. Leave to let the tea stew.

3. Scrunch up a piece of A4 paper and soak it in the cold tea mixture.

4. Leave it somewhere flat to dry (repeat for lots of pieces of paper for ongoing map making use).

5. Once dried, draw on one piece of paper a map of your setting showing the sand tray, be sure to mark an X where the treasure will be buried.

Going on a treasure hunt

1. Bury your treasure in your sand tray so it is well hidden. For extra excitement you could add plastic play trees or beach objects such as shells, coconuts and driftwood to create your own treasure island in the sand. You could even give the map to the children in a bottle and tell them you've just found it outside ... or leave it for them to find somewhere in the setting!

2. Provide children with lots of opportunities to dress up as pirates. Hats and scarves are easy to find and adapt, as are play eye patches and plastic telescopes (or cardboard tubes are even cheaper!).

3. Encourage the children to follow the treasure map to find and dig for the treasure. Enjoy reading the map together and talking about directions as you search for your treasure.

4. Using the scoops and spades, let children dig up and find the jewels. If you break up a necklace with jewel like beads, the children can sieve them out of the sand as well as the larger pieces.

Taking it forward

- Allow children access to blank treasure maps so they can make their own. If you roll them up and tie them with red ribbons like old scrolls and place in a basket they become even more exciting to a young writer or map maker!

- Bury a small box full of treasure in the outdoor sand or digging area and get children to search again.

- Provide lots of bottles, paper and pens in your water area so children can make and send their own messages in bottles.

- Have a day where just the single jewels are in the tray and children are encouraged to sieve out and sort the colours and sizes (glass beads are great for these).

What's in it for the children?

This activity in its many variations allows children to access and build on their sand handling skills at the same time as embracing imaginations and offering loads of opportunities to talk, listen and be creative.

Fizzy rainbows

What you need:

- **A shallow tray** (unused gravel or cat litter tray is ideal)
- **Bicarbonate of soda** (at least 6 domestic baking pots)
- **White vinegar and/or lemon juice**
- **Small pots** (yoghurt pots are ideal)
- **Food colouring and/or paint** (to colour the vinegar)
- **Pipettes or eye droppers**

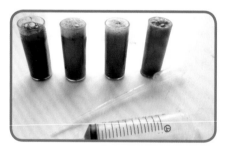

Taking it forward

- Try adding glitter to the liquid mixtures to make your rainbows really sparkle.
- Try using turkey basters and a large tray and lots of bicarbonate of soda outdoors for a big scale fizzy colour experiences.

What's in it for the children?

As well as building up children's fine motor skills by using the pipettes and droppers, this activity is lovely for exploring materials and how they change when they are mixed together.

What to do:

SKIN allergy!

1. Empty the bicarbonate of soda into a shallow tray and allow the children to explore with their fingers (it can be scooped and poured like sand).

2. Pour some white vinegar into a variety of small pots (the number will depend on how many colours you want). You can use lemon juice instead or a combination of both.

3. Add some food colouring or paint to the liquid pots until you have a rainbow of coloured liquids.

4. Use a pipette or dropper to pick up some of the liquid.

5. Squirt it on to the surface of the white bicarbonate powder and watch as it fizzes.

6. Use other colours to make fizzy rainbows and other colourful patterns.

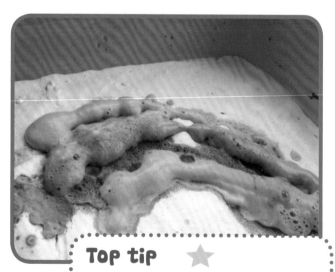

Top tip ⭐

If you can't find droppers or pipettes (they are available cheaply online) then put a drinking straw into the liquid, place your finger over the end and lift it out (with your finger still over the end). Hold the straw over the bicarb tray and let the liquid out by releasing your finger.

Sandy letters and sounds

What you need:

- A tray of wet sand
- A selection of plastic magnetic letters (preferably with the magnets removed)
- **Tools for smoothing the surface of the sand** - rulers, spatulas and windscreen scrapers etc.

What to do:

1. Mix the sand so it is wet but not soggy.

2. Smooth the surface of the sand using some of the tools provided. Some children may like to just explore this part of the activity making patterns in the sand and then smoothing them away.

3. Encourage the children to press letters into the sand and remove carefully to reveal letter prints. Talk about the sounds and encourage children to explore other sounds. Can you make you name in the sand with the letters?

4. Press a letter into the sand - can you find something in the room that starts with that letter sound?

5. Can you copy the shape of the letter in the sand with your finger?

Taking it forward

- Explore writing and mark making in the wet sand with sticks and other tools - what letters can you make in the sand?

- Bury the letters in the sand and explore initial sounds.

- Press other items into the smooth sand and see if the children can make prints (shells, upturned jelly moulds and starfish are great for this activity). If they get a really good imprint then you could place a ring of card around it, add some Plaster of Paris and make a cast of the shape.

What's in it for the children?

Making marks in wet sand allows children the chance to explore the properties of sand at the same time as building mark making skills and letter/sound recognition. A great way of using your sand tray to enhance and extend learning in other areas of learning.

Top tip ★

If you are doing this with letters remind the children to press them into the sand backwards to make sure the letter comes out the right way round!

Scented sand

What you need:

- A tray of sand
- A selection of food essences (vanilla, lemon, orange, strawberry, peppermint etc)
- A selection of chopped herbs that smell (basil, mint, lemon balm, lavender and curry plant)
- Coffee grounds

Taking it forward

- Add scented food essences to other sand mixtures like sand mousse (page 62) or quick sand (page 16) for added sensory exploration and stimulus.

What's in it for the children?

- As much as sand does not have to feel the same all the time, it also doesn't have to smell the same all the time. By adding scents to your sand as children play, you are offering more opportunities for children to extend their play and exploration using familiar materials.

- Every time young children encounter a new sensory experience they build new brain connections which play a vital part in their life long learning. Using familiar situations to enhance sensory stimulation help build on early scientific awareness as children are able to use established skills.

What to do:

1. Mix up small amounts of sand with different essences until the smell of each is distinguishable.

FOOD allergy!

2. Encourage the children to explore the sand with their sense of smell as well as their other senses as they play. You can either have lots of small amounts of smelly sand that they can mix together or use different scents on different days in your sand tray.

3. Can children tell what the smells are? Can they pick a smell that they like/dislike?

4. Let children mix chopped herbs and/or coffee grounds with sand to make their own smelly sand.

Health & Safety
Never use essential oils with children as they can cause serious allergic reactions

Volcanic eruptions

What you need:

- Wet sand in a tray or in small shallow trays
- Yoghurt pots
- Spoon
- Bicarbonate of soda
- White vinegar
- Red food colouring
- Plastic water play syringe
- Lemon juice

Taking it forward

- Why not add some dinosaurs to the sand tray for some great interactive small world play?

- Try using a mix of lemon juice and red food colouring instead of vinegar. Does it make a better eruption? Now try using a mix of both vinegar and lemon juice and see what happens.

What's in it for the children?

This activity places a popular early science experience firmly within the familiar context of childrens sand play. Once children are able to recreate the reaction themselves the exploration of materials to make mixtures of their own offers loads of problem solving and discussion opportunities alongside their independent scientific enquiry.

Top tip ★

Alternatively you can put the red vinegar mix into the pot and add the bicarb a spoon at a time.

What to do:

1. Place the yoghurt pots into the sand and build up the sand around them until they are volcano/mountain shaped with the pot sitting in the top as the crater.

2. Spoon bicarbonate of soda into the pot until it is about half full.

3. Now mix some white vinegar with some red food colouring.

4. Fill the syringe with your red vinegar mix.

5. When you are ready, squirt some of the mixture into the bicarbonate of soda and watch as your red volcano erupts out over the top of your mountain. To keep the eruption going, just keep adding more vinegar mix. When all of the bicarb is used up simply lift the pot out, rinse and begin again for hours of erupting fun.

Shells, shells and more shells

What you need:

- **A large selection of medium to large shells** in a variety of different shapes and colours
- **A tray of wet sand**

What to do:

1. Encourage children to move the sand around using only the shells. Can they fill larger shells using the smaller ones as a scoop? Can they fill the shells and make shell shaped sand castles? How many small shell scoops will it take to fill a big shell? How many small shells can they fill with a big shell full of sand?

Taking it forward

- Use really big shells for scooping sand in your outdoor sand digging area.

- Give children access to loads of different coloured and sized shells so they can explore their use in making sand patterns and creative designs.

- Invest in lots of really tiny shells that can be used in a tub as an alternative to sand for scooping and pouring.

- Allow access to large shells so children are able to explore their use as scoops and containers in sand or water play.

Top tip ⭐

Using trays with hand holes makes it easier for the children to grip.

What's in it for the children?

When playing in sand we often stick to using the old familiar equipment for scooping, digging and transporting. Sometimes by limiting what we offer and giving something slightly different we can give children more opportunity to explore these skills. Here, by offering large shells instead of scoops, spades and spoons, the children are encouraged to explore their use as alternative scooping devices. Using natural materials, encourages children to explore the open-ended use of these resources, hopefully leading to lots of imaginative talk as well as scientific and mathematical language development.

Sound sifting

What you need:

- A tray of play sand
- A selection of small objects beginning with a single phonetic sound (i.e. all items beginning with 'b')
- Scoops, spades, spoons and sieves etc

What to do:

1. Hide your selection of objects in the sand.
2. Encourage children to explore and dig up and sieve out the objects.
3. Discuss what each object is and talk about the initial sound.
4. Enjoy digging to find other objects beginning with the same sound. How many can you find? Can you bury any of your own?

Taking it forward

- Change the range of objects to explore different sounds or even blends as children become more confident (why not try objects with 'at' sounds in them?).

- Mix in some plastic letters and see if children can dig up and match the letter to the initial sound - a kind of sand snap game.

- Copy or scan pictures of objects beginning with a specific sound. Laminate the sheet and allow the children to explore independently to see if they can find everything on the 'picture list'.

- Put sand in large clear plastic drinks bottles (2 litre) and add objects beginning with a specific sound. Seal the lid with tape or a glue gun and allow children to explore finding the objects inside the bottle by pouring and shifting the sand around inside.

What's in it for the children?

An excellent opportunity to build on childrens existing sand handling skills by scooping, digging and sieving to find the sounds. An excellent example of using your sand provision as a stimulating focus for learning in other areas. A great one for building on co-operative skills as children work together to find the objects.... Oh and of course it builds phonics understanding!!

Scoop it up!

What you need:

- Sand
- Water
- Empty ice cream tubs
- Food colouring
- Food essences
- A selection of ice cream scoops
- Foam ice cream cones (made by cutting a circle of coloured foam and then shaping into a cone and gluing)

What to do:

1. Mix up some sand and water until it is wet but not too soggy (sandcastle texture).

2. Divide the sand up into separate plastic containers.

3. Add different food colours to each of the tubs and mix until you get a really nice ice cream colour.

4. Add enough food essence to be able to smell the sand for each 'flavour'.

5. Enjoy scooping up the sand and making different ice cream cones.

6. Encourage children to explore the scents and the colours and to talk about and create their own flavours.

7. Add glitter sprinkles for added effect.

Taking it forward

- Encourage the children to incorporate the 'scooping sand' activity into role-play and create your own ice cream shop. Remind them to write the flavours and prices for their customers!

- What colours does it make when you mix your coloured ice creams together?

- Add lots of different sized scoops (ice cream, melon scoop, measuring scoop, ladle etc) to coloured and natural wet sand play.

- Use the coloured sand to make sand jellies by pressing into jelly moulds.

- Use soup ladles to scoop sand on a bigger scale outdoors. Can you make giant ice creams?

What's in it for the children?

As well as lots of sensory exploration with both scents and colours as part of the sand play, this is a lovely activity for promoting mathematical language such as counting: 'How many scoops?' 'One more', 'One less' etc. Using the scoops (especially if you can get one with a thumb press release) will help to build those all important motor skills in hands, wrists and fingers.

Sand mousse

What you need:

- 1 bottle of washing up liquid
- A tray of play sand
- Warm water
- A selection of cups, spoons, scoops and funnels

SKIN allergy!

What to do:

1. Squirt a large amount of the washing up liquid on to the sand (at least half a bottle).

2. Add small amounts of water and stir as you go.

3. Stir until the sand has frothed up into a smooth mousse like texture.

4. Explore with hands, spoons, cups and funnels etc.

Taking it forward

- Add colour to the mix (green makes a great swampy mix for crocodiles etc).

- Add scents such as orange, lemon or peppermint food essence for a multi-sensory exploration.

- Add some sequins or glitter to the mix for added sparkly appeal.

- Add some sand mousse to a large shallow tray (a gravel garden tray is ideal or even a washing up bowl or a paddling pool) and allow children to explore with their feet either indoors or outdoors.

What's in it for the children?

Many children only get the chance to explore sand in its natural state. To be able to build their knowledge of familiar materials as part of early scientific exploration it is important to offer children lots of variants of sand to be able to build sensory experiences and early understanding of how materials behave. This mixture gives and unusal chance to stimulate senses whilst children pour, scoop and squish the mousse.

Sieving for gold

What you need:

- **Wet sand in a tray or in small shallow trays**
- **Water**
- **A selection of sieves** (metal and plastic)
- **Gold-coloured decorative gravel** (available from garden centres)

What to do:

1. Make up the sand and water mixture until it is really sloppy.

2. Stir in the gold stones.

3. Now encourage children to use the sieves to find the gold in the sand.

4. For added excitement and imagination, give the children small pouches to put their gold in once they have found it (little organza bags used for wedding favours are great for this!)

Taking it forward

- Add some glass beads and sieve for jewels as well as gold.

- Add even more water to the mix to make a sand and water tray combined so children can really pan for gold in the water (especially if the tray is outside on the floor like a river). Outdoors you can use big garden soil sieves to get your gold out of the sand.

What's in it for the children?

Enhancing everyday provision to make it even more appealing and exciting is a must if children are to actively engage with learning opportunities. This is a great way of developing scooping, sieving and pouring skills whilst embracing an exciting challenge. Lots of opportunities to talk imaginatively about the search for gold and your finds as well as building early maths language with talk of 'full', 'less', 'more' and counting of gold stones.